ASTONISHING X-MEN

UNSTOPPABLE

writer_**JOSS WHEDON**

artist_**JOHN CASSADAY**

colorist_**LAURA MARTIN**
letterers_**CHRIS ELIOPOULOS**
WITH **JOE CARAMAGNA**

assistant editors_**SEAN RYAN & WILL PANZO**
associate editor_**ANDY SCHMIDT**
editors_**MIKE MARTS & NICK LOWE**

collection editor_**JENNIFER GRÜNWALD**
assistant editors
_**CORY LEVINE & JOHN DENNING**
editor, special projects_**MARK D. BEAZLEY**
senior editor, special projects
_**JEFF YOUNGQUIST**

senior vice president of sales_**DAVID GABRIEL**
vice president of creative
_**TOM MARVELLI**

editor in chief_**JOE QUESADA**
publisher_**DAN BUCKLEY**

PREVIOUSLY:

The oracles of Breakworld foresaw a future where their world was destroyed by a mutant from Earth. So they sent one of their own, ORD, to take care of the problem. His solution was to develop a "cure" for mutancy that would eliminate the danger to his homeworld. In the process of creating this "cure," Ord resurrected the deceased X-Man COLOSSUS to be used as a research subject.

The X-Men stopped Ord from wiping out the Earth's mutants and he was then incarcerated by S.W.O.R.D. (Sentient Worlds Observation and Response Department), an organization led by AGENT BRAND. Irony reared its ugly head when S.W.O.R.D. precognitives discovered that the mutant destined to destroy Breakworld was the mutant Ord brought back to life — Colossus.

Ord broke out of S.W.O.R.D. imprisonment with the help of the sentient robot DANGER, and attacked the X-Men, who, at the same time, were falling apart at the seams. EMMA FROST, under the influence of CASSANDRA NOVA and suffering from extreme survivor's guilt, mentally took apart the X-Men. They were able to save their teammate and themselves, but not without consequence. CYCLOPS lost his optic blasts and KITTY PRYDE is still suffering from the emotional anguish Emma caused her.

All of this was thrown on the back burner as S.W.O.R.D. has just teleported Ord, Danger and the X-Men (along with X-student HISAKO) aboard a starship.

IT'S A LOCALIZED GRAVITY SURGE, ACTUALLY. HANDY FOR UNRULY PASSENGERS.

AGENT BRAND...YOU'VE GOT TEN SECONDS... TO TURN THAT... OFF...

OR WHAT?

OR ELSE.

THIS KID'S NOT A KILLER.

YOU HAVE NO IDEA WHO I AM.

GONNA PUT A BULLET IN MY HEAD?

FOR STARTERS.

ANYBODY STARTS ANYTHING-- I'M LOOKING AT YOU, ORD--AND I'LL TURN THE GRAV SO HIGH IT'LL LIQUIFY YOU.

LET 'EM UP.

POWERLORD KRUUN. THIS MESSAGE IS URGENT.

IT COMES FROM?

AMBASSADOR ORD.

ORD.

THE STINK OF HIS INCOMPETENCE WILL OUTLAST HIS BODY'S DECAY.

AS YOU SPEAK IT, IT COMES TO PASS.

RRZZTTP KRLORD KRUUN. URGEKKTZ.

LORD OF MY WORLD. I HAVE LITTLE TIME.

I'M ABOARD A S.W.O.R.D. WARSHIP ON DIRECT SLING TO THE BREAKWORLD. SILATYN HAS OUR COORDINATES.

PAIN...

SEVEN GODS, THIS PAIN...

I NOTICE YOU'RE NOT SPORTING THE SHADES.

YEAH. I'VE LOST ACCESS TO MY POWER.

FROST DO THAT?

IT'S COMPLICATED.

I GOT A LOTTA VARIABLES ON THIS MISSION ALREADY. IF SHE'S A DIRECT THREAT--

AGENT BRAND, EMMA FROST IS AN X-MAN.

AND?

I'M UNAWARE OF THE NEED FOR A CONJUNCTION.

YOU ALWAYS TALK LIKE THAT?

EMMA'S ONE OF US. THAT MEANS SHE'S--

NOT HERE.

CASSANDRA NOVA IS NOT HERE.

THE MIND IS CLOUDED...

YOU KIDNAPPED US.

WE'RE NOT PAST THAT YET?

IT WAS FOUR HOURS AGO.

THE MOMENT THE AUGURS PINPOINTED RASPUTIN, AN ARMADA WAS SENT TOWARDS EARTH.

ON THE WAY TO HIS CELL, ORD BROKE FREE AND CONTACTED THE BREAKWORLD.

THAT ARMADA IS NOW HEADED TOWARDS US.

JUST LIKE YOU PLANNED.

JUST LIKE I PLANNED.

I WONDERED WHY YOU WERE SO SPECIFIC ABOUT OUR COORDINATES IN FRONT OF THE GUY.

I NEEDED TO DRAW THEM AWAY FROM EARTH. NOW THE BEST WAY TO KEEP THEM FROM BLOWING THIS SHIP INTO FRAGMENTS IS TO GET TO THE BREAKWORLD BEFORE THEY CAN.

AT CURRENT SPEED, WE SHOULD JUST MAKE IT.

THIS PLAN SEEMS OVERWHELMINGLY FLAWED, AGENT BRAND.

REFUGE IN THE LION'S MOUTH? WON'T EVERY LIVING SOUL ON THE BREAKWORLD BE LOOKING TO PUT PETER DOWN?

YOU THINK I HAVEN'T THOUGHT OF THAT, COOKIE MONSTER?

WHEN ARE YOU GUYS GONNA FIGURE OUT THAT THIS IS BIGGER THAN ALL OF YOU?

WHEN YOU FIGURE OUT WHO YOU'RE DEALING WITH, YOU SILLY BINT.

SORRY I'M LATE. I THINK I PICKED THE GIST OF IT UP ON THE WAY.

ALTHOUGH AGENT BRAND DID FORGET TO MENTION THAT SHE'S TERRIFIED.

NOT OF YOU.

THE BREAKWORLD IS GOVERNED BY ONE PRINCIPLE: DOMINATION. BY VIOLENCE, WAR, EXTERMINATION...

POWERLORD KRUUN, OF THE OPEN HAND. THE GLOBAL RULER OF THE BREAKWORLD. HIS RISE TO POWER DID NOT, YOU'VE PROBABLY GUESSED, INVOLVE AN ELECTORAL COLLEGE.

AND HE'S WHAT YOU'RE AFRAID OF.

OH HOW I WISH.

SPLINTER IS UP FOR THRUST, YOUR COMMAND.

TIME TO THE BREAKWORLD?

FOURTEEN MINUTES TO CLEAN ORBIT.

TIME TILL THE SHIP IS SHREDDED?

A LOT LESS.

EVERYBODY HANG ON TIGHT.

"UNBREACHABLE HULL, PRECISE MANEUVERABILITY, ENOUGH POWER AT SHORT-RANGE TO OUTRUN ANYONE."

PRETTIEST SHIP IN THE FLEET.

NOT TO BE PICKY, AGENT BRAND, BUT IF THIS SPLINTER IS SUCH A WONDERFUL SHIP...

WELL, WE GOT YOUR SIZES RIGHT.

THE BREATHERS GO BEHIND YOUR TEETH. THEY'LL FILTER OUT IMPURITIES, AND THE CAPSULES WILL TIME-RELEASE SUPPLEMENTARY OXYGEN.

EARWIGS WORK AS TRANSLATORS.

WE RENDEZVOUS AT THE GLOWING RED DOT. THE G.P.S. MAPS'LL GUIDE YOU, BUT IF YOU LOSE 'EM, YOU'RE LOOKING FOR ATTUR-HEI.

"PALACE OF THE CORPSE?"

GOOD, IT'S WORKING.

YES, IT'S VERY IMPRESSIVE. PALACE OF THE CORPSE?

IT'S A TOMB, GOT DUG UP RECENTLY. OUR SOURCE ON THE BREAKWORLD SAYS IT MIGHT TIE IN TO THE RASPUTIN PROPHECY.

WE HAVE A SOURCE?

WE CAN'T DO ALL THIS NOW.

WE GET ON THE WORLD, WE FIND OUT HOW RASPUTIN'S SUPPOSED TO BE A THREAT, VISIBLY NULLIFY THAT THREAT AND TAKE OUT THE MISSILE THEY'VE GOT POINTED AT THE EARTH.

MORE QUESTIONS WHEN WE'RE ON-WORLD.

MS. PRYDE HAS VERY LONG ARMS.

SO...

...WHICH OF US IS "FLOTSAM"?

STILL READING LIFE-FORMS, COMMANDER.

BELAY KILLSTRIKE.

PREPARE TO BOARD.

KID'S OUT.

HOW YOU RIDIN', KITTEN?

WALK IN THE PARK.

I WORRY... ABOUT THE OTHERS...

IT'S VERY THOUGHTFUL OF YOU, EMMA.

WELL, GOOD LORD, WHY SHOULD WE ENDURE ALL THAT CENTRIFUGAL NONSENSE? TWO LUMPS, DEAR.

WE CAN ALL "LIVE IN THE NOW" ONCE WE'RE ON SOLID GROUND.

I JUST WANNA MAKE SURE YOU'RE NOT OVERDOING IT, HONEY.

ALSO, IF WE START TO DIE, WE SHOULD PROBABLY KNOW.

WE WON'T DIE.

THE METAL--
LIKE ORD'S SHIP,
IT'S...
I
CAN'T...

HE FELL FROM THE SKY HOLDING A HUMAN GIRL. PEOPLE GATHERED TO SEE AND MOMENTS LATER THEY SANK RIGHT INTO THE EARTH.

WE'RE CERTAIN THIS WAS COLOSSUS?

THE PEOPLE WERE. THEY PANICKED. AND IT SPREADS. THEY BELIEVE HE'S GONE INTO THE EARTH TO INFECT IT.

THAT THE PROPHECY HAS BEGUN.

AND FOR ALL WE KNOW THEY COULD BE RIGHT.

IT DOESN'T FIT EXACTLY, BUT THIS IS NOT AN EXACT SCIENCE. WE COULD HAVE MISINTERPRETED THE ATTUR-HYN.

LET'S HOPE THE PRISONERS HAVE SOMETHING USEFUL TO SAY.

IT'S THE GIRL.

THIS IS HER POWER: TO MOVE THROUGH SOLID OBJECTS. COLOSSUS WILL BE SOMEWHERE ABOVE GROUND. HE CAN BE STOPPED.

BUT NOT BY YOU.

I AM THE ENGINE OF OUR DESTRUCTION. I REQUEST ONLY THAT MY DEATH BE PAINFUL AND PUBLIC.

DOUBT IT NOTHING. YOU DRAW BREATH ONLY AS LONG AS YOU MIGHT BE OF USE.

SYLATIN, WHAT OTHER CAPTIVES HAVE WE?

SEVERAL SOLDIERS FROM THE WRECK OF THEIR SHIP, MOSTLY HUMAN. ONE SYNTHETIC, CLAIMS SHE WAS HELPING ORD.

IMAGINE THAT.

HE NEEDED HELP EVEN TO FAIL.

WHAT OF THE SMALLER VESSEL? DID OUR HUNTERS FIND IT?

A FORCE IS MINUTES AWAY.

IT WAS NO DOUBT A DIVERSION, BUT I WANT THE SOLDIERS CAPTURED ANYWAY. ALL INFORMATION IS VALUABLE, SO ONLY KILL THE NECESSARY EXAMPLES.

I'LL TALK TO THE SYNTHETIC.

START BREAKING THE OTHERS.

YOU'RE NOT READY TO SEE ME, KID.

I DON'T THINK WE SHOULD BE STAYING IN ONE PLACE. WE'RE NOT FAR ENOUGH FROM THE CRASH TO BE SURE...

THAT ARMOR'S PRETTY DAMN IMPRESSIVE. HIT THE GROUND WITHOUT A SCRATCH.

CAN'T SAY THE SAME FOR MY FACE.

ANOTHER HALF-HOUR, I SHOULD HAVE SOMETHING RESEMBLING A NOSE. AND SOME TENDONS. THEN WE MOVE.

I HAVE A TEST ON WEDNESDAY.

I'M NOT AN X-MAN, I SHOULDN'T...I MEAN I CAN'T--

I HAVE A CHEMISTRY TEST.

NOBODY HEARD.

GOD...WHAT IS THIS WORLD MADE OF?

PETE?

PETER, WE HAVE TO KEEP MOVING.

TO WHAT?

TO THE TOMB, THE ATTUR-HEI PLACE. SEE WHAT THEY DUG UP--

AND THEN? REGROUP, MAKE PLAN, COMMIT GENOCIDE, GO HOME?

NO.

PETE, NO. WE'RE NOT FALLING FOR THAT.

THESE PEOPLE READ THE FUTURE.

THEY SEE ME DESTROYING THEM. AND THE AGENT, BRAND, SHE AS MUCH AS TELLS ME TO.

AND THE DAY WE TAKE ORDERS FROM HER IS THE--

I WAS MILLIONS OF MILES AWAY, KATYA. AND DEAD.

AND NOW?

WE WILL FIND ANOTHER WAY.

"THERE'S NO SET FUTURE, PETER. I KNOW THAT AS WELL AS ANYONE.

"JUST BECAUSE THEY SAY YOU'RE A DANGER TO THIS WORLD..."

"...DOESN'T MEAN IT'S WRITTEN IN STONE."

21

PETE AND KITTY?

THEY HAVEN'T SHOWN YET. BUT THEY'RE ALIVE: NEWS IS REPORTING A LOT OF SIGHTINGS.

WHAT *HAPPENED* TO YOU LOT?

AGENT BRAND'S BRILLIANT PLAN WENT SOUTH. OUR PRETEND BURNING WRECKAGE STOPPED PRETENDING.

WE GET THROUGH THIS, I'M GONNA POP A CLAW THROUGH HER EYE, YOU GUYS COOL WITH THAT?

ABSOLUTELY.

LOGAN, WE DON'T JUST... NAH, GO FOR IT.

WELL. THIS DOESN'T LEAVE A WHOLE LOTTA ROOM FOR DOUBT, DOES IT?

HOWZIT WORK? IS THAT THE SUN?

BEST GUESS.

SO, WHAT? SUPERNOVA, ORBITAL SHIFT?

VERY LIKELY, MS. ICHIKI. HIGH MARKS FOR THE STOWAWAY STUDENT.

I'M NOT... I HAVE A NEW, UH...

SHE'S CALLED "ARMOR". SHE'S OUR NEW TEAMMATE.

I MEAN, THAT IS...LOGAN SAID.

OH, IT'S LOVELY. GOD KNOWS THE TEAM'S GOING TO NEED SOME NEW BLOOD SOON.

DID HE TEACH YOU THE HANDSHAKE?

WITHOUT A LAB, I CAN'T REALLY TELL MUCH ABOUT THIS CARVING.

THE SYMBOLS ARE OLDER THAN ANYTHING IN OUR BANKS. GONNA BE A WHILE BEFORE WE GET SPECIFICS.

I THINK WE OUGHTA SPLIT UP.

AT LAST WE AGREE ON SOMETHING.

YOU'RE COMING WITH ME.

AND SO ENDS THAT ERA.

I NEED TO GET A LOOK AT THE WEAPON THEY'VE GOT POINTED AT THE EARTH. THERE'S A BASE DIRECTLY UNDER ITS ORBIT A HUNDRED MILES EAST. YOU'RE SCIENCE DIVISION, SO YOU COME WITH.

I WANNA FIND PETE AND KITTY. I'LL TAKE THE KID.

AREN'T YOU SUPPOSED TO CALL ME--

I'M INTERESTED IN THIS KRUUN.

YOU'RE NOT UP TO FACING HIM.

I'VE GOT MEN IN THE FIELD, I THINK YOU AND MS. FROST SHOULD RENDEZVOUS WITH THEM AND WAIT FOR WORD.

IS THAT WHAT YOU THINK.

NO OFFENSE, BUT YOU'RE POWERLESS AND SHE'S MORE THAN NORMALLY UNSTABLE. I WASN'T COUNTING ON EITHER OF THOSE THINGS WHEN I BROUGHT YOU HERE.

WANT ME TO POP THAT CLAW?

NO.

LADY HAS A POINT.

LET'S DO THE WORK.

ARE WE DONE HERE?

KILL IT!!!

RASPUTIN AND PRYDE. YOU WILL COME WITH US.

IT'S UNLIKELY.

YOUR TRANSLATORS ARE PRIMITIVE.

IT IS NOT AN ORDER.

WE ARE ASKING.

WE ARE ASKING FOR YOUR TRUST.

I AM UNIMPRESSED.

WE ALREADY HAVE INTELLIGENCE ON THE X-MEN.

NOT LIKE MINE. I WAS CREATED TO KILL THEM.

AND YET THEY LIVE.

I WAS DISTRACTED. BY A MORE IMPORTANT MISSION.

AND I WAS YOUNGER THEN.

I DON'T CARE ABOUT YOUR WORLD ANY MORE THAN YOU CARE ABOUT ME. BUT OUR INTERESTS COINCIDE.

THE X-MEN CAN BE STOPPED.

POWERLORD, WE HAVE WORD FROM THE ATTUR-HEI.

COLOSSUS?

HIS CONFEDERATES. AND AGENT BRAND--THEY OVERCAME THE GUARDS, BUT ONE WOKE TO SEE THEM GO THEIR SEVERAL WAYS.

IF THIS MACHINE IS RIGHT, THEY KNOW ABOUT THE RETALIATOR. IT MUST BE PROTECTED.

BRING DOWN A SNOWSTRIKE BETWEEN ATTUR-HEI AND THE SUB-MOON BASE.

AND THOSE HEADED ELSEWHERE...?

WHAT WILL YOU NEED?

WHY EXACTLY DID YOU RESCUE US?

OH, I HAVEN'T RESCUED YOU; THIS IS POSSIBLY THE MOST DANGEROUS PLACE ON THE PLANET.

IF POWERLORD KRUUN KNEW A THING ABOUT IT, THIS MOUNTAIN WOULD BE A CRATER.

I SOUGHT YOU OUT BECAUSE I BELIEVE YOU MAY BE THE INSTRUMENT OF OUR SALVATION.

YOU DON'T BELIEVE THE PROPHECY?

I DIDN'T. AND THEN YOU WERE HERE.

AND I THOUGHT PERHAPS IT'S NOT THE PROPHECY THAT'S WRONG, BUT THE INTERPRETATION.

A WORLD IN CHAOS, PERHAPS, BUT NOT DESTROYED. RE-FORMED.

REBORN.

I AM NOT A MESSIAH.

BY THE WORLD, *NO*; YOU'RE A MAN.

BUT YOU'VE BEEN THRUST INTO THE ARENA, WILLING OR NO. THE WORLD IS WATCHING.

I'VE BEEN IN THE ARENA. A SHOW-KILLER; THAT'S WHAT I WAS BRED AS.

THE THRONG SCREAMS AND YOUR HEAD CROWDS WITH ONLY TWO CHOICES: KILL, BE KILLED. I WON SO OFTEN THE ROAR BECAME LIKE THE AIR TO ME. I COULDN'T EVEN HEAR IT.

AND IN THE SILENCE, THE THIRD CHOICE CAN BE HEARD.

I HAVE NO AGENDA FOR YOU. NO PLAN, NO COUP.

I BROUGHT YOU HERE SO YOU COULD HAVE A MOMENT TO HEAR THAT GREAT SILENCE, UNDERSTAND THAT THIRD CHOICE. TO KNOW THAT EVEN ON A WARRIOR WORLD, WE CAN BE MADE TO UNDERSTAND IT TOO.

WE CAN BE BETTER.

REST TONIGHT.

AND TOMORROW YOU DO WHAT YOU WILL.

CONFUSED?

YOU THINK I CANNOT PIERCE A DIAMOND?

OH, HAVE I HARDENED? DEFENSE MECHANISM; QUITE UNCONSCIOUS.

THERE NOW. BETTER?

THIS IS A TRICK.

HUSH NOW. KILL AWAY.

KRUUN WILL WANT YOU ALIVE.

NONSENSE. HE'LL BE THRILLED. SHOWER YOU WITH GARLANDS AND WEAR MY SKIN LIKE A SHAWL.

WHAT GAME ARE YOU PLAYING?

OH, I'M A TERRIBLE PERSON AND I'M WRACKED WITH GUILT, HAVEN'T YOU BEEN FOLLOWING?

IF YOU SHAKE HARDER MY NECK MIGHT SNAP... IF THAT HELPS AT ALL...

SHALL I TELL YOU WHY YOU HAVEN'T KILLED ME YET?

I DID NEED KITTY TO EXPLAIN THE MECHANICS, BUT YOU WERE PROGRAMMED TO KILL US AND THEN SADDLED WITH A "PARENT PROGRAM" THAT STOPPED YOU.

THE ROGUE SENTINEL, THE ALLIANCE WITH THAT NON-WIT, ORD... DESPERATE ATTEMPTS TO GET SOMEONE TO DO WHAT YOU STILL CAN'T.

EMMA... GET BEHIND ME...

WHY I FIND SUCH PATENTLY IDIOTIC CHIVALRY A TURN-ON IS TRULY A MYSTERY TO ME. BUT YOU, "DANGER"...

YOU'RE AN OPEN BLACKBERRY.

YOU NEVER GOT OVER YOUR PARENT PROGRAMMING.

IF IT'S ANY CONSOLATION, NOBODY EVER DOES.

UM...CAN I GET KIND OF A SIT-REP HERE?

I'M ABOUT TO MAKE OUR DREAD ARCH-NEMESIS AN OFFER.

AND I'LL BET SHE CAN GUESS WHAT IT IS.

I MADE JOKES.

WE NEED A SHIP.

IT'S A NATURAL ENOUGH RESPONSE, I SUPPOSE, TO UNIMAGINABLE HORROR--

LET'S THINK DEEP THOUGHTS LATER, PROFESSOR. THERE *WILL* BE SURVIVORS AND WE *DON'T* WANT TO MEET THEM.

WE NEED TO RAID THAT SHIPYARD AND GET TO THE DAMN MOONBASE.

I THINK NOT.

SO THE MACHINE FAILED ME AS WELL.

THE X-MEN ARE GATHERED. ON A TRANSPORT SHIP. IT CAME OUT OF THE STRIKE-QUAD HALF-FROZEN, A BORDER DROID CLICKED ON THE ANOMALOUS HEAT SIG.

LUCK, THEN.

THERE'S MORE.

WHEN THE X-MEN RENDEZVOUSED, COLOSSUS AND SOME OTHERS WERE RECORDED WITH AN UNREG.

ONE OF AGHANNE'S.

GRRAAHNNGGH!!

THAT WOMAN IS MORE DANGEROUS THAN A HUNDRED PROPHECIES.

IF HER MADNESS SPREADS...

THE TRANSPORT HAS EYES FOR US?

OH YES.

SHOW ME.

YOU PUT THAT *THING* IN CHARGE OF MY MEN?

CAN SHE POSSIBLY DO A WORSE JOB THAN YOU?

DRAGON!

I CAN'T BELIEVE YOU GOT DRAGGED INTO THIS TOO! WHERE HAVE YOU BEEN HIDING?

IT'S A KILLING MACHINE!

TECHNICALLY...

DIDN'T YOU SAY YOUR MEN WERE EXPENDABLE? IN MY MEMORY, YOU SAID THAT.

WHAT'S WRONG? ARE YOU HUNGRY, LITTLE FELLA?

OH FOR GOD'S SAKE, STOP SIMPERING AT HIM!

LOCKHEED WORKS FOR US.

HE'S BEEN DOING SURVEILLANCE ON YOUR TEAM SINCE YOU REJOINED.

WOW.

YOU'RE SO UNPLEASANT EVEN *I'M* IMPRESSED. DO YOU VISIT ORPHANAGES TO EXPLAIN THERE'S NO SANTA?

THIS IS EXACTLY YOUR PROBLEM! INFANTILIZING ALIEN RACES...

...THAT DRAGON SPEAKS MORE LANGUAGES THAN THE PROFESSOR; HE'S NOT SOME STARLET'S CHIHUAHUA.

LOCKHEED HAS SOME HOMEWORLD ISSUES WE'RE HELPING HIM WITH.

PRESSING ISSUES.

BRAND, YOUR FILES SHOW NO MENTION OF THIS "AGHANNE".

WELL, NO, OF COURSE. IF WHAT RASPUTIN SAYS ABOUT HER IS TRUE, SHE'LL HAVE BEEN EXPUNGED.

I'M AMAZED SHE'S ALIVE AT ALL.

COMING UP ON THE MOON...

WELL, WE NEED TO TALK TO HER.

DISTURBING LACK OF SECURITY...

IF HER INTERPRETATION OF THE PROPHECY IS TRUE...IF PETER IS SOMEHOW INVOLVED IN SAVING THIS RACE...

I DON'T KNOW. THE KID AND I HAVE BEEN SEEING THIS PLACE AT GROUND LEVEL...

STILL NOT CALLING ME "ARMOR"...

...I KINDA LIKE THE VERSION WHERE PETE BLOWS IT UP.

OKAY, PEOPLE, WE GOT MORE BAD NEWS...

WE EXPECTED THE MOON TO BE FORTIFIED. YOU DON'T THINK WE CAN LAND?

YOU KNOW, I THOUGHT I'D HAVE A LOT MORE FUN IF I EVER GOT TO SAY THIS...

SAY WHAT?

"MAKE ME PROUD."

I WAS NOT YET ENTIRELY OUT OF FAVOR THEN. NOW IT WOULD BE SUICIDE FOR THEM TO HELP US. WE MUSTN'T JUDGE.

THAT'S NOT WHAT THE PRYDE GIRL SAID.

TOLD THEM OUR SAD HISTORY, HAVE YOU?

THEY ASKED ABOUT YOU. ARE THEY NOT ALLIES? SHOULD I NOT--

NO, IT'S FINE. IT JUST EXPLAINS THIS SPARK IN YOU. ALREADY WE CHANGE IN THEIR THRALL.

ANY CHANCE IS BETTER THAN KRUUN'S MURDEROUS MADNESS.

UNTHINKING BRUTALITY DOES NOT MAKE ONE MAD, DAFI...

ONLY HOPE CAN DO THAT.

THE X-MEN WILL COME WHEN THEY CAN. THEY HAVE LOST A SOLDIER TODAY...

THAT'S FINE, SURE.

EMMA.

WHAT WE DID BACK THERE, I'M... I'M NEVER GONNA BE OKAY WITH THAT--

AND YOUR APPROVAL IS NECESSARY FOR...?

THAT'S NOT THE POINT. I JUST THOUGHT...

...THAT I MIGHT NEED TO TALK?

OH YES, LET'S *TALK*--LET'S SHARE OUR FEELINGS AND HAVE SLUMBER PARTIES AND TRY ON HATS.

YOU UNDERSTAND ME SO *TERRIBLY* WELL.

YEAH, HILARIOUS ME; I THOUGH YOU MIGHT ACTUALLY FEEL SOME KIND OF LOSS.

I AM A DIAMOND, MS. PRYDE.

I AM, BY DEFINITION, MY OWN BEST FRIEND.

SO THAT'S WHAT THAT'S LIKE.

HAVE YOU LOOKED THE WORD "SUPERHERO" UP? LIKE, GOOGLED IT OR SOMETHING?

THAT AIN'T THE MISSION.

AAHHH!!!

LOGAN!

CLIK

HOW SO?

THIS PROPHETIC ROCK, WITH PETER DESTROYING THE BREAKWORLD...THE STONE IS ANCIENT, AS IS THE EARTH IT WAS PULLED FROM.

BUT THE CARVING PATTERN, THE PRECISION...

I'D GUESS IT WAS DONE WITH A LASER.

WE DON'T KNOW HOW FAR BACK BREAKWORLD TECHNOLOGIES REACH.

NO, WE DON'T.

WHAT WE DO KNOW IS HOW IT'S SUPPOSED TO GO DOWN.

I CAN'T READ THIS.

THE KEY ON THE RIGHT. TRANSLATION.

YOU CAN READ THIS.

I'VE STUDIED THIS RACE FOR A WHILE. PICKED UP SOME LANGUAGE.

YOU SPEAK IT?

ENOUGH TO ORDER A STEAK. HIT THE DAMN KEY.

SO. THIS IS THE WAY THE WORLD ENDS.

YOU'RE NOT AFRAID OF PAIN.

BUT YOU CAN'T BE NAÏVE ENOUGH TO THINK THAT PAIN IS MY ONLY WEAPON.

A HUMAN MAN CAN ONLY WATCH SO MANY PARTS OF HIMSELF REMOVED BEFORE HIS MIND GOES.

NOT JUST YOUR LIMBS, CYCLOPS. ORGANS, SKIN...I CAN KEEP YOU ALIVE IN A JAR.

"AND THEN THERE'S YOUR X-MEN. CAN YOU STAND TO WATCH ME WORK ON THEM?"

"THE ONE WHO HEALS IS PROBABLY TOO VOLATILE, AND RECORDS INDICATE YOU MIGHT NOT MIND A LITTLE DISCOMFORT IN HIS CASE."

"BUT THE NEW ONE, THE YOUNG WOMAN..."

"WILL YOU WATCH HER PICKED APART?"

WHERE IS AGHANNE.

WHERE IS COLOSSUS.

AND WHAT. IS. LEVIATHAN?

GOODNESS!

FORGIVE US. WE WERE DETECTED AND HAD TO TRAVEL THE LAST FEW MILES WITHIN THE GROUND.

PHASING SOMETHING SO BIG, SO FAR... AND YOUR... EARTH...

KATYA!

I KNOW NOTHING OF HUMAN HEALING...

THE MATERIALS IN YOUR EARTH ARE HARMFUL SOMEHOW.

TINGLING... OOH...

YOU SHOULD NOT HAVE PUT YOURSELVES IN SUCH DANGER TO COME TO ME.

WE HAD NO CHOICE, AGHANNE.

YOU CAN'T JUST HAVE ME CALLED ME "SWEETIE."

YOUR WITCH IS NEARBY.

IT WILL AVAIL YOU NOTHING-- SHE CANNOT BREACH THESE WALLS.

THEY'RE NICE WALLS. WOULD YOU LIKE ME TO START ANSWERING YOUR QUESTIONS NOW?

"PETER--COLOSSUS-- IS WITH AGHANNE. SHOULD BE ON THEIR WAY."

BUT YOU ORDERED HIM--

--TO STAY AWAY FROM HER, HOW COULD YOU HAVE KNOWN THAT OH MY GOD DID YOU HAVE SOME KIND OF *SURVEILLANCE* DEVICE ON YOUR OWN SHIP THAT WE STOLE?

YOU KNEW I WAS WATCHING.

EMMA, HELP ME.

I, UH...

RIGHT. I'M LINKING YOU ALL PSYCHICALLY. TRY TO KEEP TALKING NORMALLY.

WE NEED TO GET CLOSE TO KRUUN. THAT WON'T HAPPEN UNLESS HE THINKS WE'RE HELPLESS.

SO I'LL TAKE THE REPAIR SHIP AND GET MYSELF CAPTURED.

THERE'S A GOOD CHANCE THEY'LL KILL YOU, BOSS.

SUPP... THE LEADER.

THEY'RE GAINING...

THAT'S WHY I'M ACTING LIKE ONE.

THEY BROUGHT PETER BACK TO LIFE. THEY'LL DO THE SAME WITH ME IF THEY THINK I HAVE INFORMATION THEY NEED.

A SECRET WEAPON?

THAT WOULD WORK...

WE NEED A NAME: SOMETHING OMINOUS AND IMPOSING.

OUR ACE IN THE HOLE.

LEVIATHAN?

OH, HONEY, THAT'S IRRESISTIBLE! "LEVIATHAN."

KRUUN'LL WORK ME OVER FOR A WHILE TRYING TO GET THAT OUT OF ME. THE REST OF YOU GET TO WORK.

EMMA, I'LL NEED SCHEMATICS OF THE PRISON. LOGAN AND HISAKO, GET YOURSELVES CAPTURED IN A FEW HOURS SO WE'VE GOT A FORCE INSIDE.

I OBJECT!

WHAT?

BUGGER ME, WAS THAT ACTING?

IS NOT COURTROOM DRAMA, KATYA.

GONNA ... YOU ...

SHUT UP! I'M NOT GOOD AT HAVING TWO CONVERSATIONS AT ONCE. AND I HATE SCOTT'S PLAN!

YOU MEAN YOU "OBJECT" TO IT. BUT I'M GONNA ALLOW IT.

S#!%. I'M GONNA CRACK UP. I'M CRACKING UP.

SAY SOMETHING CYNICAL.

RIGHT. RIGHT.

EXCUSE ME, I'M THE ONE WHO'S GONNA

AGENT BRAND, YOU AND HANK WORK THAT PROPHECY. PETER, BRING AGHANNE INTO THE FOLD IF YOU CAN. BE OUTSIDE THE PRISON IN A FEW HOURS. BRING EVERYONE.

STA... KR... FR... EVE...

EMMA ...

I'D BETTER GO BEFORE KITTY TRIES TO ACT AGAIN.

SCOTT, IF KRUUN HAS YOU AT HIS MERCY...

DON'T WORRY, MY LOVE...

"LEVIATHAN" WILL SAVE ME.

HANK, YOU GET KITTY TO THE MISSILE. IF THE TWO OF YOU CAN'T DISABLE THAT THING, IT CAN'T BE DONE.

I'LL MAKE SURE THEY GET THERE SAFELY.

NO YOU WON'T.

AGENT BRAND KNOWS THE TERRAIN SO SHE'S IN. LOGAN AND ARMOR ARE THE ESCORT.

SCOTT--

NOT ASKING, PETE.

YOU'RE OUR ACE IN THE HOLE. YOU CAN ACTUALLY DO THE THING KRUUN FEARS MOST. KILL THE PLANET.

IT'S UGLY, BUT IT'S A CARD WE GOTTA HOLD.

AGHANNE AND EMMA ARE WITH US. REST OF YOU ARE HOLDING THE FORT. MAKE A BIG NOISE OF IT; THE MORE FORCES YOU DRAW HERE THE BETTER CHANCE EVERYONE ELSE HAS.

OUR BOYS GOT WORKED OVER PRETTY BAD. WE'RE READY FOR SOME FIREWORKS.

APPRECIATED. QUESTIONS?

I NEED A MINUTE ALONE.

WE DON'T KNOW HOW MUCH TIME--

NOT ASKING, SCOTT.

SIR.

I HATE THIS PLAN.

NOT JUST THE PART WHERE I CAN'T TOUCH YOU FOR THE NEXT TWELVE HOURS; I HATE THE *PLAN.*

SCOTT'S PUTTING YOU RIGHT WHERE THE PROPHECY SAID YOU'D BE. DON'T LET THINGS GET OUT OF YOUR CONTROL.

I AM AN X-MAN, KATYA. I AM NOT IN THE BUSINESS OF DESTROYING PLANETS.

ESPECIALLY WHEN I AM ON THEM.

SCOTT WOULD RATHER KEEP YOU CLOSE, BUT I THINK YOU'LL BE OF MORE USE TO THE AWAY TEAM.

STOP THAT MISSILE OR...WELL, THERE ISN'T MUCH OF AN "OR" FOR ANYONE, IS THERE?

I DON'T FEAR ANNIHILATION AS YOU DO. I JUST WANT TO BE SURE YOU WON'T GO BACK ON YOUR WORD WHEN WE'RE DONE.

YOU'RE PROGRAMMED TO KNOW ME BETTER THAN THAT. HELP US SAVE THE WORLD...

...AND I'LL GIVE YOU CHARLES XAVIER.

IT MAKES NO SENSE. TO PUT YOUR WORLD AT RISK WITH SUCH A FRAGILE, UNSTABLE ENERGY SOURCE...

WE PRIZE EFFICIENCY OVER SAFETY. IS IT VERY DIFFERENT ON EARTH?

NOT AS MUCH AS WE'D LIKE. SHALL WE BEGIN? I BELIEVE HE'S WAKING UP.

NO...

THIS IS VERY SIMPLE.

OUR WORLD FOR YOURS.

YOU DON'T KNOW WHAT YOU'VE DONE.

WE HAVEN'T DONE ANYTHING YET. DISABLE YOUR MISSILE AND WE FADE AWAY. YOU'RE THE HERO THAT SAVED THE BREAKWORLD.

THE RETALIATOR WILL FIRE AS SCHEDULED. NOTHING YOU DO CAN STOP IT.

SERIOUSLY: ARE YOU TRYING TO WIPE OUT YOUR WORLD?

ISN'T IT?

YOU GOT SOMETHING TO SAY TO ME?

SCADS.

IT'LL HAVE TO SIT. WE GOT THIRTY VESSELS MOVING TO INTERCEPT. I THOUGHT THE POWERLORD'S PRIVATE RIDE WOULD SLIP US THROUGH, BUT THEY MUST'VE GOT WORD. WE NEED A PLAN.

LADY KEEPS TALKING LIKE SHE'S IN CHARGE...MAKES MY KNUCKLES ITCH.

I'M LOOKING FOR SUGGESTIONS, ALL RIGHT?

LAST TIME, SUMMERS PUT HIMSELF IN A RESCUE CRAFT AND DIED TO KEEP US FROM GETTING TAGGED. YOU GOT THE STONES FOR THAT?

HOW CAN I NOT KILL THESE MORONS...?

RELAX. THE INTERCEPTING CRAFT ARE FALLING BACK. THEIR COMPUTER SYSTEMS THINK THEY'RE FAILING.

YOU'VE INTERFACED? CAN YOU ACCESS THE MISSILE?

OR?

NOTHING. IT'S NOT NETWORKED, OR...

EMMA, MOVE!

AT LAST, THIS ENDS AS IT WAS MEANT TO.

OH, PLEASE.

AHH!

IT IS OVER!

I THINK NOT.

FOR YOUR WORLD, IT IS.

THE RETALIATOR FIRES IN SECONDS.

IT CANNOT BE STOPPED.

NOTHING.

I'VE GONE MORE...THAN AN MILE...

NO WIRES, NO WORKS... I...

THIS METAL...

WHAH!

THERE'S A SPACE NEAR THE TOP, BUT NO DAMN CONTROLS!

HOW THE HELL DO THEY GUIDE THIS THING?

RRRRRMMMMMM

RRRRRRRRRRRMMMMM

SHE'S FIRING!

OH NO... NO...

GIANT-SIZE 1

WOW. I ALL OF A SUDDEN FORGIVE YOU.

IT IS COMING SOON, AND WE DIDN'T WISH YOU TO BE STARTLED.

I WAS GONNA LAND ON MY FEET, FYI, AND IF YOU DON'T WANT TO STARTLE A GUY DON'T TELEPORT IN HIS FACE A HUNDRED FEET ABOVE THE CITY.

YOU COULD MAYBE TEXT.

ENTSCHULDIGEN SIE, BITTE.

NO, I'M ONLY FORGIVING HER.

SHE DIDN'T MEAN STARTLED BY US, WEB-BUTT.

FUNNY. NOT "HA-HA" FUNNY, BUT...

OH. STARTLED.

NOW I GET IT.

NOT SURE I WANT IT...

YOU GET THIS MANY BIG GUNS IN ONE ROOM NOT CIVILLY WARRING, IT'S EITHER THE END OF THE WORLD, OR...

... I DON'T HAVE AN "OR".

ORORO.

GOOD TO SEE YOU. IS THE PROFESSOR HERE?

NOT INVITED. NO ONE WILL SAY WHY.

THE MUTANTS ARE KEPT IN THE DARK, AS ALWAYS. IT'S OUR PEOPLE OUT THERE--

OUT WHERE?

--AND STILL THEY TELL US NOTHING.

THEY WILL TELL ME.

ANNND, SHRINKAGE.

FELLOW HEROES! WE ARE ALL ASSEMBLED.

IF WE ARE TO ACT, WE MUST ACT IN CONCERT.

WHAT HAS HAPPENED?

AND TO THINK, I WASTED CONCERN.

WE SHOULD BE GOING AFTER KITTY.

WE CANNOT CATCH UP IN THIS VESSEL.

SCOTT AND EMMA ARE *EN ROUTE*, IN KRUUN'S FASTEST SHIP. WE NEED TO BACK UP PETER.

PETE SHOULD DO THE JOB AND GET OUT.

TELL ME I DIDN'T JUST HEAR YOU SUGGEST GENOCIDE.

WHAT DO YOU THINK THEY'RE TRYING TO DO TO *US*?

SUMMERS GETS CLOSE ENOUGH, HE CAN BOUNCE A MESSAGE TO THE PEAK, GET SOME OF EARTH'S MIGHTIEST HEROES WORKING THIS FROM THE OTHER END.

WE NEED TO TAKE ONE LAST SHOT AT KRUUN.

I CAN KILL HIM, RIGHT?

I GOT SOMETHING MORE DIPLOMATIC IN MIND.

PETER DOESN'T KNOW, DOES HE?

HE DOESN'T KNOW ABOUT KITTY.

COME ON...

I CAN'T BE *THAT* WEAK...

"WE'VE LOST CONTACT WITH THE PEAK."

WE'RE SUDDENLY GETTING STATIC. AND YOU'RE BARELY SINGED.

SORRY I DIDN'T *DIE* TAKING THE HIT FOR YOU, PROFESSOR.

FIVE MINUTES TO DROP, PEOPLE.

YOU'RE KEEPING SOMETHING FROM ME.

MY FRIENDS-- MY *WORLD*--AT STAKE, AND YOU'RE STILL HIDING SOMETHING.

IT AIN'T RELEVANT.

I'LL DECIDE THAT.

IT'S PERSONAL.

AND HERE I AM IN YOUR PERSONAL SPACE SO GO AHEAD AND OPEN UP.

I AM SO HOT FOR YOU RIGHT NOW I COULD FRIKKIN' PASS OUT.

TOLD YOU IT WAS PERSONAL.

"BULLSEYE."

ANOTHER X-MESS
CLEANED UP BY THE
EVER-LOVIN' FOUR.

WE STILL HAVE
TO SAVE KITTY
PRYDE...

USING ONE OF
MY OLD TIME-
CONDENSERS, WE'LL
BE ABLE TO GET TO
HER SECONDS AFTER
SHE ENTERED THE
NEGATIVE ZONE.

BLAH-DE-
SCIENCE-BLAH.
WE SAVED THE
WORLD, REED!

TAKE A
MOMENT TO
ENJOY IT.

WE THROW EVERYTHING AT IT, IT WOULDN'T ALTER COURSE.

HELL, WE *RAM* THE THING WE'D JUST BE A BUG ON A WINDSHIELD.

UNLESS YOU'VE GOT A NOTION, EMMA, IT'S UP TO THE OTHERS.

EMMA?

KITTY?

EMMA?

KITTY. IT'S ALL RIGHT. HELP IS ON THE WAY.

SO DID THEY.

"THERE IS A WAY TO STOP THE MISSILE."

IT IS NO MERE MISSILE--

MY FRIENDS HAVE TOLD ME.

EVERYTHING.

AGENT BRAND SAYS THAT A POWERLORD CAN NEVER RETREAT, CAN NEVER CREATE A CONTINGENCY FOR AN ATTACK.

BUT THERE IS A WEAKNESS. IN THE DESIGN, SOME SMALL GLITCH, AND YOU WILL KNOW OF IT.

YOU WILL TELL US WHAT THE WEAKNESS IS. NOT OUT OF ANYTHING AS DISTASTEFUL AS COMPASSION.

YOU WILL TELL ME BECAUSE YOU KNOW THAT EVEN IF MY WORLD IS ENDED, I WILL NOT DESTROY YOURS.

AAAHGHHH!!

I WILL *RULE* IT.

MY PEOPLE WOULD NEVER...

YOUR PEOPLE FEAR ME AS THEY NEVER WILL YOU. I AM THE DESTROYER.

AND ACCORDING TO AGENT BRAND, I HOLD THE SYMBOL OF YOUR SERVITUDE IN MY HAND. YOUR TIME IS DONE.

WE LOSE THE EARTH, WE'RE GONNA NEED A PLACE TO CRASH. FOREVER.

YOU'RE NOT POWERLORD ANYMORE. YOU NO LONGER BEAR THE BURDEN OF HIS SECRETS. SO UNLESS YOU WANT YOUR WORLD OVERRUN BY A HOST OF VERY UNHAPPY SUPERPEOPLE, USE YOUR NEW FREEDOM.

WHAT IS THE WEAKNESS?

YOU CAN'T WAKE ANYONE?

THE MOST POWERFUL SEEM TO BE THE MOST POWERFULLY HIT. SPIDER-MAN IS STILL TRYING TO ROUSE DR. STRANGE...

AT LEAST, I THINK THAT'S WHY HE'S HITTING HIM...

ORORO, WE'RE GETTING VERY CLOSE. WE'VE BEEN TOLD THAT A DIRECT HEAD-TO-HEAD HIT BY SOMETHING BIG ENOUGH MIGHT BUCKLE THE BULLET, OR AT THE VERY LEAST DIVERT IT.

IT'S GOT TO BE DEAD ON.

AND IT'S GOTTA BE SOON.

SOUNDS GREAT.

SOUNDS REALLY GREAT.

KITTY... I... I CAN PUT YOU SOMEWHERE ELSE.

I CAN MAKE YOU LESS AFRAID.

NAH. NAH, I'M GONNA SEE THIS THROUGH.

PETER SHOULD KNOW...WELL, HE SHOULD ALREADY KNOW, SO DON'T WORRY ABOUT IT.

THIS WAS NEVER MEANT TO...NOT YOU.

YEAH, I WAS SUPPOSED TO TAKE YOU OUT, AS I RECALL.

DISAPPOINTED, MS. FROST?

ASTONISHED, MS. PRYDE.

"YOU DON'T MEAN
SHE'LL NEVER
COME BACK."

I GUESS I'LL START.

I'M FAIRLY CERTAIN I HATE YOU.

WELL, THAT'S KIND OF THE POINT.

I NEED SOMEONE TO HATE ME. PROFESSIONALLY. I'M GOOD AT--WELL, I'M UNIQUELY QUALIFIED FOR-- MY JOB.

BUT I MADE SOME CRAP CALLS THIS TIME AROUND, AND WE BOTH LOST MEN WE SHOULDN'T HAVE.

YOU'RE SMARTER THAN ANY DOZEN GUYS AND YOU'LL QUESTION MY EVERY WAKING GESTURE. ON THE JOB, THERE'S NOTHING I COULD USE MORE.

AND OFF THE JOB?

PRETTY MUCH WANNA BREAK YOU LIKE A PONY. IT'S A WIN-WIN.

I'M A BLUE FURRY MONSTER.

SO WAS MY FATHER.

I'VE GOT GREEN HAIR, WHICH I DID NOT DYE. I SPEAK OFFWORLD LANGUAGES THE HUMAN TONGUE CANNOT FORM. I GOT HOT, GLOWY HANDS, AND I RUN THE MOST IMPORTANT SECURITY ORGANIZATION IN OUR SYSTEM WITHOUT BENEFIT OF SOCIAL SKILLS OF ANY KIND.

I'M AN ALIEN, GENIUS.

ON MY FATHER'S SIDE.

THIS IS A HARD TIME FOR YOU, SO I'M NOT GONNA PUSH, BUT...

THE SAFETY OF THE ENTIRE PLANET PROBABLY RESTS ON YOUR DECISION AND YOU AND I ARE COMPATIBLE IN WAYS YOU DON'T HAVE WORDS FOR, SO...

...SO I'M NOT GONNA PUSH.

"I THINK YOU HAVE TO GRAB IT WHILE YOU CAN.

"YOU TAKE WHAT YOU CAN GET.

"'CAUSE IT'S HERE, AND THEN..."

GONE

WHEDON CASSADAY MARTIN

19 VARIANT

20 VARIANT

21 VARIANT

23 VARIANT